To all children

Invincible generators of chaos

Never-ending inventors of fantastic realities

Sharp observers

With millions of whys always ready for us

In continuous struggle with their emotions and rebellious to the point of exhaustion

Small universes of originality capable of constantly surprising us

Wonderful little concentrates of happiness

Each one different

All of them special

Can I cook by myself?

CAN I COOK by MYSELF?

Step-by-step recipes for KIDS cooking ON THEIR OWN +4

Francesca
MUSCI

Gabriel Marco
LONGATO

Author and illustrator

Chef and source of inspiration

Can I cook by myself?

CAN I COOK by MYSELF?

a picture of me

This book belongs to

My age

Date

SUMMARY

RECIPES

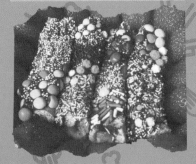

INTRODUCTION

The recipes in this book have been chosen and adapted to make children as independent as possible and to transform preparing meals into a fun, formative and conscious activity. Children will be able to exercise their manual skills, have fun experimenting, gain confidence in their abilities and share happy times with their families.

The ingredients that are used are simple, easily obtainable and usually loved by children.

Each recipe can be personalized, feel free to consult the suggestions, in the ingredients tabs. You can make any changes you want in case some ingredients are not liked or your children want to experiment with new combinations.

Oven baked methods are preferred to make cooking healthier and to avoid using the stove as much as possible. For safety reasons always take charge of the cooking yourself.

The preparation of these recipes are designed for children as young as 4 years old, but they will need your support with some of the steps.

You should prepare in advance the work surface, the ingredients and the necessary tools so that the children will be able to easily follow the recipes and procedures.

The receipts used are visual and sequential in order to help children, even the youngest, who do not yet know how to read, to recognize the ingredients and carry out the creations as independently as possible.

Preparation times are approximate and each child has their own pace. Oven temperature and baking times are also approximate depending on your oven and the size of the pans used.

HAVE FUN

SYMBOLS

 Preparation time

 Oven Cooking

 Put in the refrigerator

 Microwave cooking

 Oven or microwave temperature

 Bring the water to boil

 Materials suitable for microwave cooking

 Materials suitable for cooking in the oven

 Cooking times

 Boil water in the Kettle

 Yogurt pot of 125 grams

 Ideas for alternative ingredients

 Help needed from an adult

 Adult only activities

 Danger: baking

 Danger: microwave cooking

 Danger: Knife use

 Danger: burns

Tips for adults

This recipe is very flexible, you can change the ingredients with the ones you like the most. You can add more flavor with spices, herbs or a few extra pinches of salt.

Let the tartlets cool before removing them from the mold to avoid breakage.

A fresh spinach and cucumber salad is great to accompany this dish.

Egg TARTLETS

 20 min   200°C/392°F   20 min

Ingredients for 6 tartlets

Eggs — 4

Parmesan cheese — 4 🥄

Salt — 3

Extra virgin olive oil — 2 🥄

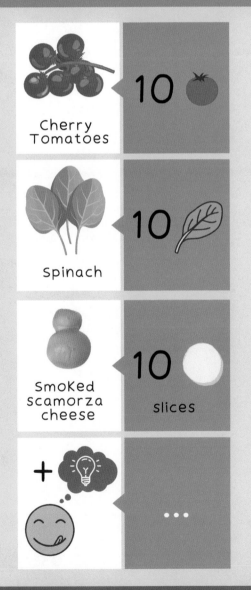

Cherry Tomatoes — 10 🍅

Spinach — 10 🌿

Smoked scamorza cheese — 10 slices

+ 💡 ... 😋

20 min 200°C/392°F

ENJOY!

Tips for adults

This dish is fresh and delicate and can be enriched with other ingredients according to your taste.

Be careful when cutting and emptying the tomatoes, the children will need your help. A sharp knife is necessary; the children could cut themselves and the tomatoes could break.

In the recipe, the olives are left whole, but it may be necessary to cut them up. Evaluate this according to the age of your children to avoid choking hazards when eating them.

Wait a few hours before serving these tomatoes to let them take on flavor and make them even tastier.

Serve them cold or at room temperature, do not reheat them.

Couscous
TOMATOES

30 min

Ingredients for 6 tomatoes

Couscous — 3 (cup)

Tomatoes — 6

Salt — 12 (pinch)

Extra virgin olive oil — 6 / 2 (spoons)

Canned chickpeas — 12 (spoon)

Pitted olives — 6 (spoon)

Parsley / sprigs — 2

Lemon — 1

Water — 2 (cup)

15

3

2  **2**

boiling water

6

3

1

2

12
6

 **6** 1 teaspoon for each tomato

 **6** 1 pinch of salt in each tomato

enjoy!

Let's play together

What you need for this recipe

Tips for adults

The cannelloni used in this recipe are the dry ones that can be found in many supermarkets; for better cooking the tomato sauce must not be too thick and it is advisable to add some spoons of milk.

If you have some ready made sauce, cannelloni will be tastier, otherwise raw tomato puree will be just as good.
Spinach must be well drained before adding it to the ricotta mixture in order not to water down the filling.

Filling the cannelloni with the mixture is not very easy for children because it requires manual skill and patience. To facilitate the process use the handle of a teaspoon to push the dough into the cannelloni; repeat until they are completely filled.

For the filling you can substitute the spinach with the ingredients that your children like the most. Look in the suggestions for alternative ideas.

Make a single layer of cannelloni, if necessary divide them into two pans.

Ricotta & Spinach CANNELLONI

40 min   200°C/392°F   40 min

Ingredients for 6 servings

Dry cannelloni — 22

Tomato puree — 6

salt / Extra virgin olive oil — 15 / 3

Milk — 1/2

Ricotta cheese — 2

Spinach — 450 grams or 12

Béchamel sauce — 10

Parmesan cheese — 10

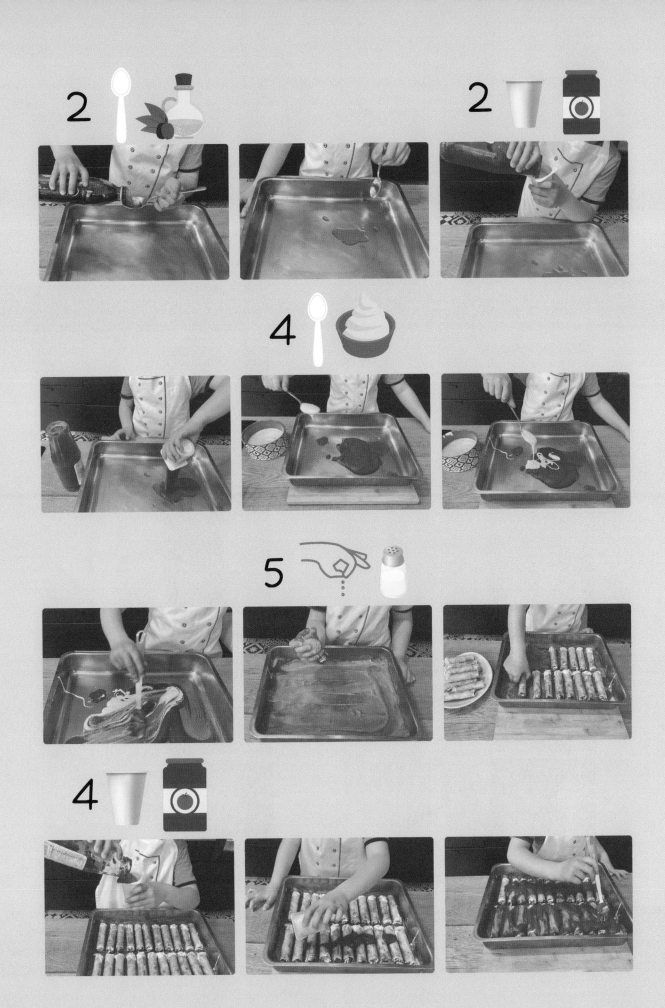

5

1/2

6

4

40 min   200°C/392°F

enjoy!

Let's play together

25

Tips for adults

For this recipe you can choose the bread you want and according to this you may need to adjust the quantities of the ingredients so that the bread slices are well soaked with the mixture made with the egg and milk.

In order to make the slices crispy on both sides it is necessary to turn them halfway through baking; changing the baking paper if the mozzarella has released too much liquid.

If instead of baking you prefer to fry, as in the original recipe, leave out the milk or reduce it by half.

Mozzarella in Carrozza should be crispy on the outside and soft on the inside with a melted filling.

You can accompany this recipe with a fresh salad of spinach, cherry tomatoes and cucumbers.

Mozzarella in CARROZZA

30 min   215°C/419°F   15 min

Ingredients for 6 servings

 Mozzarella — 2

 Eggs — 8

Salt — 10

Extra virgin olive oil — 1

Milk — 8

Bread — 12 slices

+ ...

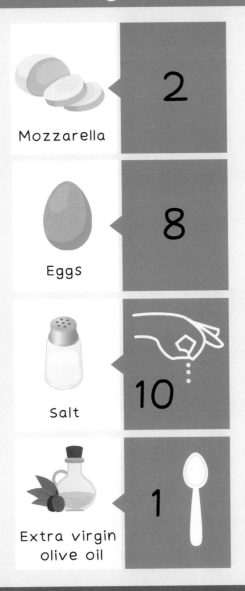

8

1

10

8

2

12

 30 min   215°C / 419°F

enjoy!

Tips for adults

You can boil the rice or use leftover risotto from other dishes. Use rice suitable for risotto so that it does not become runny and the grains remain well separated.
Calculate the cooking time of the rice according to the instructions on the package, taking care to drain it when al dente; it will finish cooking in the oven.

Children should be accompanied in cooking the rice and adults should take care upon draining.

Place Risottini directly onto the plate, using a flat spatula to hold under the molds.

You can accompany this recipe with baked potatoes and green beans.

BaKed RISOTTINI

 20 min   210°C/410°F   20 min

Rice for risotto — 3

Tomato puree — 16

Coarse salt — 3

Extra virgin olive oil — 2

Smoked scamorza cheese — 1

Peas — 10

Parmesan cheese — 10

Water — 12

12

3

al dente

16

10

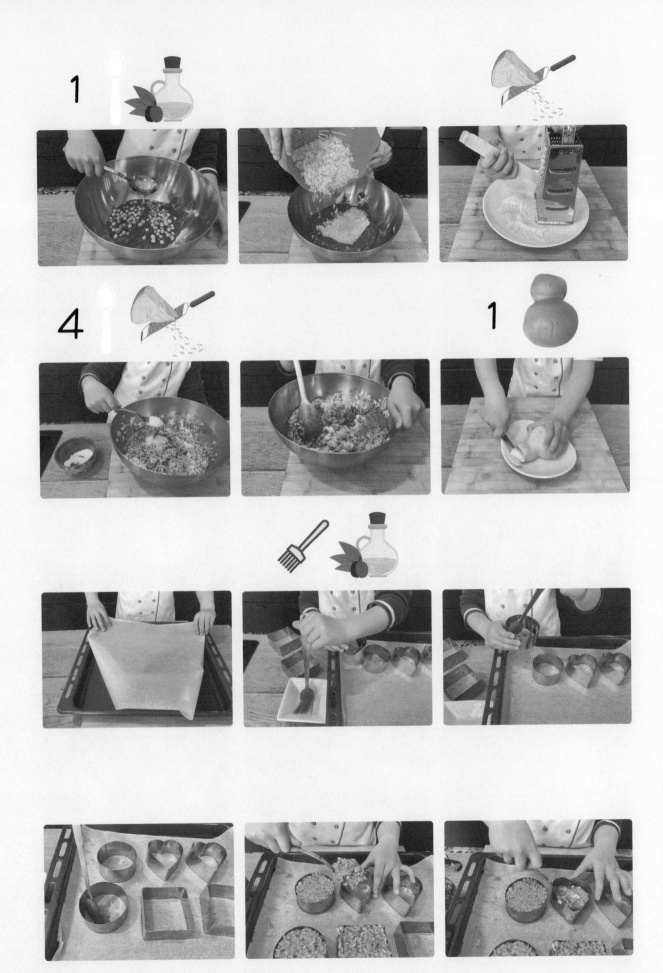

6

20 min   210°C/410°F

enjoy!

Let's play together

What you need for this recipe

Tips for adults

Baked potatoes are a great complement to many dishes and kids love them.

Buy organic potatoes so you can leave the skin on, it will be easier for the children not to have to peel them.

Leave the garlic in its skin so it gives the aroma to the potatoes and not the pungent taste; remove it before serving the potatoes.

If you don't want to eat the rosemary, leave the sprigs whole and remove them when serving the potatoes.

The amount of potatoes to calculate per serving varies according to their size. Generally, medium-small potatoes are more manageable for children; choose the quality you like best and adjust cooking times according to your oven and size of the chunks the children cut.

Turn the potatoes halfway through cooking to achieve the gold browning on all sides.

BaKed POTATOES

 40 min   220°C/428°F°   10 min

Ingredients for 6 servings

18 Organic potatoes

2 sprigs Rosemary

Salt **8**

4 Extra virgin olive oil

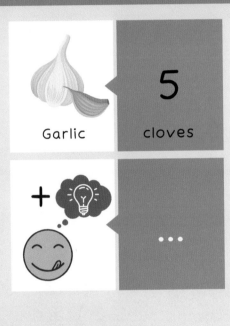

Garlic **5** cloves

+ ...

 + → ...

18 🥔🥔

8 🧂   **3** 🥄🫒   **5** 🧅

2 🌿

🖌️🫒

40 min 220°C/428°F°

enjoy!

What you need for this recipe

For pesto sauce

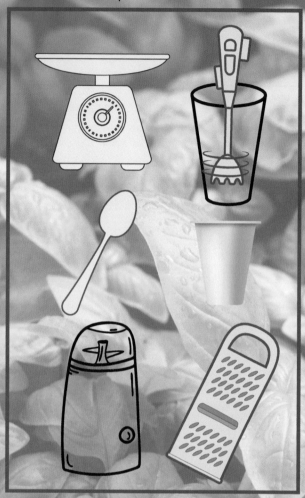

For pasta

Tips for adults

Basil pesto can be customized to your taste; you can substitute the cashews for pine nuts, almonds, pistachios and leave out the garlic or parmesan if desired.

Use an ice cube to blend with the basil and other ingredients it will give the pesto a bright green color and creamy texture.

Trofie pasta with
PESTO

 boiling

 20 min

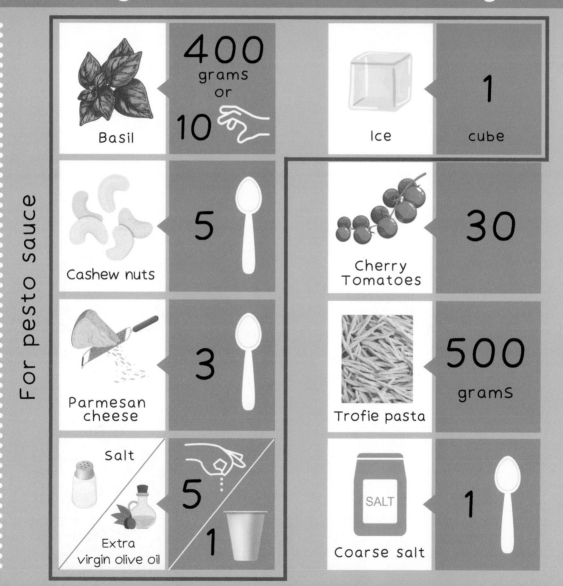

For pesto sauce

Basil — **400** grams **or** **10** 🤏

Cashew nuts — **5** 🥄

Parmesan cheese — **3** 🥄

Salt / Extra virgin olive oil — **5** / **1** 🥛

Ice — **1** cube

Cherry Tomatoes — **30**

Trofie pasta — **500** grams

Coarse salt — **1** 🥄

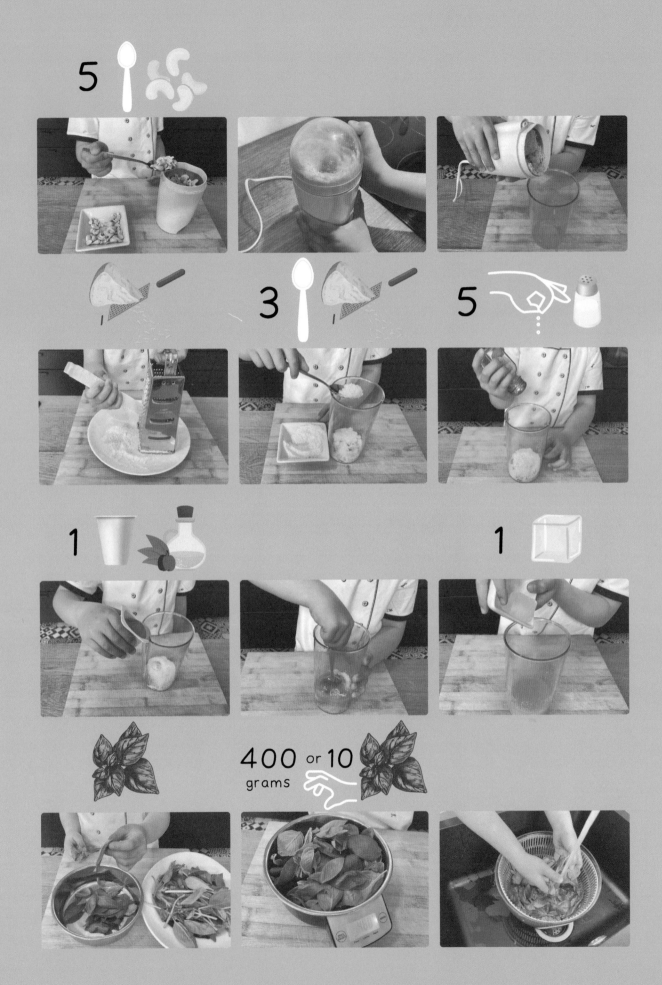

30

2

1 SALT

500 grammi

 al dente

enjoy!

Let's play together

45

What you need for this recipe

Diameter:
25 cm / 9,84 inch

Tips for adults

This zucchini puff pastry is super simple and very tasty.
For better cooking place it in the lower part of the oven.
Adjust the cooking time according to your oven, be careful with
the bottom of the puff pastry that may not cook perfectly, in
which case you can rest the pan on the bottom of the oven
during the last 5 minutes. Be careful not to burn it.

This dish is also great served at room temperature and
accompanied with baked potatoes.

Zucchini
PUFF PASTRY

 40min   180°C/356°F   15 min

Ingredients for 6 servings

 Zucchini — 2

Smoked scamorza cheese — 1

 Parmesan cheese — 6

 Puff pastry — 1

+  ...

2

1
1

1

1/2
3

1 **1/2** **3**

40 min 180°C/356°F

enjoy!

What you need for this recipe

Tips for adults

Parmesan cheese is optional in this recipe; you may leave it out if you don't like the taste of cheese in the breadcrumbs.

Crispy, baked asparagus is a tasty dish to serve as an appetizer or side dish.

You can use the same technique for other crisp vegetables.

Crispy ASPARAGUS

 30 min 200°C/392°F 20 min

Ingredients for 20 asparagus

Asparagus — 20

Plane Flour — 1

Parmesan cheese — 3

Extra virgin olive oil — 4

Salt — 3

Bread crumbs — 12

Eggs — 2

+ ...

20

Flex the asparagus until they break apart

Eliminates the hard part

Preserves the soft part of the stem

Dry the asparagus

1

Plate no.1 **1**

2

3

Plate no.2   ②

12 🥄 🍚

🧀 3 🥄🧀 4 🥄🫒

Plate no.3   ③

🥢 ① 🥢 ② 🥢 ③

53

30 min   200°C/392°F

enjoy!

Let's play together

What you need for this recipe

For Cocoa Hazelnut Cream

For Fantasy Rolls

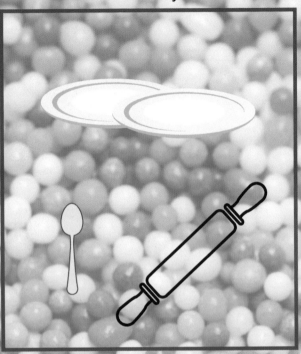

Tips for adults

For the cocoa hazelnut cream use a sugar free organic hazelnut butter, it can be found in most supermarkets.

Instead sugar in the recipe it is recommended to use Erythritol: a natural sweetener with almost zero calories that does not decay teeth and taste similar to sugar. Erythriol does not dissolve easily so it is necessary to grind it to a fine powder to avoid the grainy texture in desserts that do not require baking.

This cream is great for so many uses and you can store for several days out of the fridge in a closed jar.

Spread the slices of bread with the types of jam you prefer for example those with reduced sugar content or those containing agave syrup.

Fantasy
ROLLS

20 min

Ingredients for 4 rolls

For Cocoa Hazelnut Cream

Hazelnut butter	**350** grams
Erythritol sweetener	**6** 🥄
Cocoa	**2** 🥄
Bread	**4**

Jam	**4** 🥄
Topping of your choice	**6** 🥄
😋	**+** 💡 ...

6 🥄 ▦

1 🥄 🫙

enjoy! 😋

What you need for this recipe

Tips for adults

Chocolate salami is a very simple but really tasty and versatile dessert.

You can use the chocolate you like best and add dried or candied fruit to your liking.

If only using dark chocolate you must add some powdered sugar or Erythritol to avoid the flavor be too bitter.

Take the chocolate salami out of the refrigerator about 15 to 20 minutes before serving it so that it is easier to cut the slices without breaking them.

You can put a slice of chocolate salami in a sandwich for the children's snack or serve it accompanied by a scoop of ice cream and fresh cream as an after meal dessert.

Chocolate SALAMI

5 hours   **15 min**

Ingredients for 6 servings

Milk chocolate — **170** grams

Dark chocolate — **30** grams

Cocoa — **1** 🥄

Dry biscuits — **10**

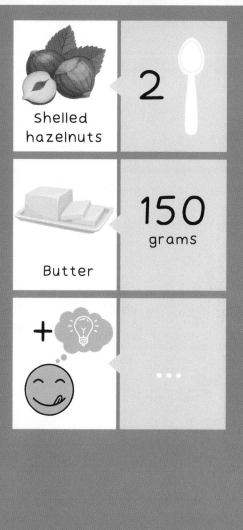

Shelled hazelnuts — **2** 🥄

Butter — **150** grams

+ 💡 😋 — ...

150 grams

170 grams

30 grams

3 min **650W**

1

5
hours

enjoy!

Let's play together

LOOK AT WHAT'S ON THE PLATES AND
SET THE TABLE PROPERLY

What you need for this recipe

Diameter:
25 cm / 9,84 inch

Tips for adults

This fruit cake doesn't need to be baked, is very fresh and delicate, and is suitable for customizing with your kids' favorite fruit and jam. Erythritol is used In the recipe (a natural sweetener, almost no calories that does not decay the teeth and with a taste similar to sucrose) if you prefer you can use powered sugar.

If you want to give a firmer consistency to the cream you can boil a few tablespoons of lemon juice with a teaspoon of
agar-agar (a natural vegetable gelatin) and add it to the cream once it has cooled.

Make sure the fruit has been thoroughly dried before decorating to prevent the water from running into the cream of the cake.

Fruit CAKE

3-4 hours   **50 min**

Ingredients for 8 servings

Dry biscuits	**28** (300 grams)	Erythritol sweetener	**5**
Butter	**150** grams	Lemon	**1**
Cream cheese	**12** (500 grams)	Wild berries	as you want
Fresh cream	**2**	Blueberry jam	**3**

 + →   ... 😋

28
(300 gr)

150 grams

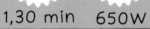
1,30 min   650W

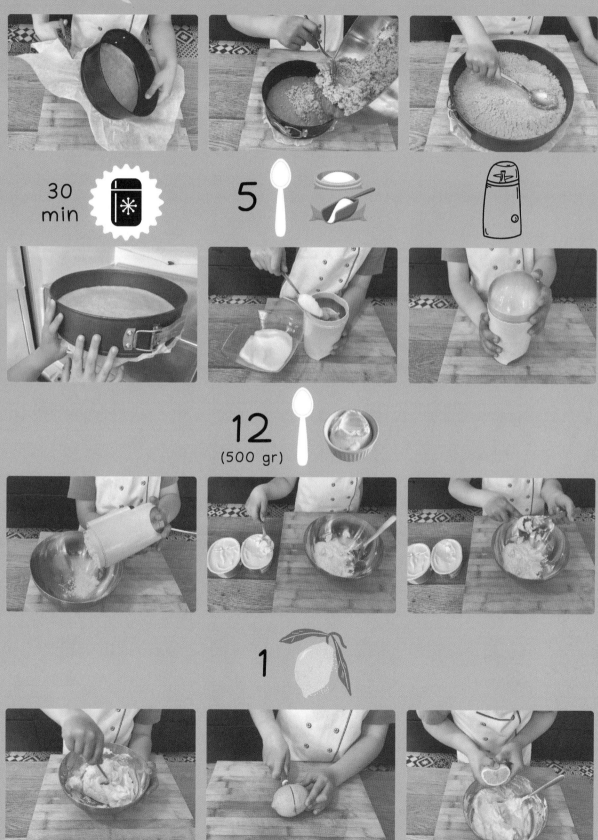

wash the fruit

dry gently the fruit

wash the fruit

dry gently the fruit

enjoy!

FIND THE INTRUDER

Pag. 19

HOW MANY APPLES WITH THE WORM ARE THERE?

Pag. 25

8

FIND THE 10 DIFFERENCES

Pag. 35

HELP OUR FRIENDS FIND OUT WHO STOLE A SLICE OF PIZZA

Pag. 45

THE CUCUMBER HAS LOST ITS WAY TO GO INTO THE SALAD, CAN YOU HELP HIM?

Pag. 55

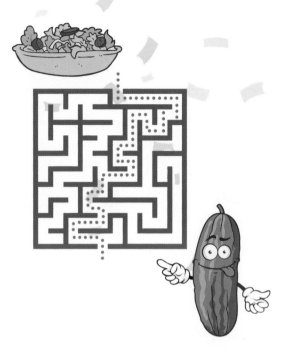

THIS TABLE HAS BEEN SET WRONG: FIND ALL THE MISTAKES

Pag. 65

LOOK AT WHAT'S ON THE PLATES AND SET THE TABLE PROPERLY

Pag. 65

MY
PICTURE

MY
PICTURE

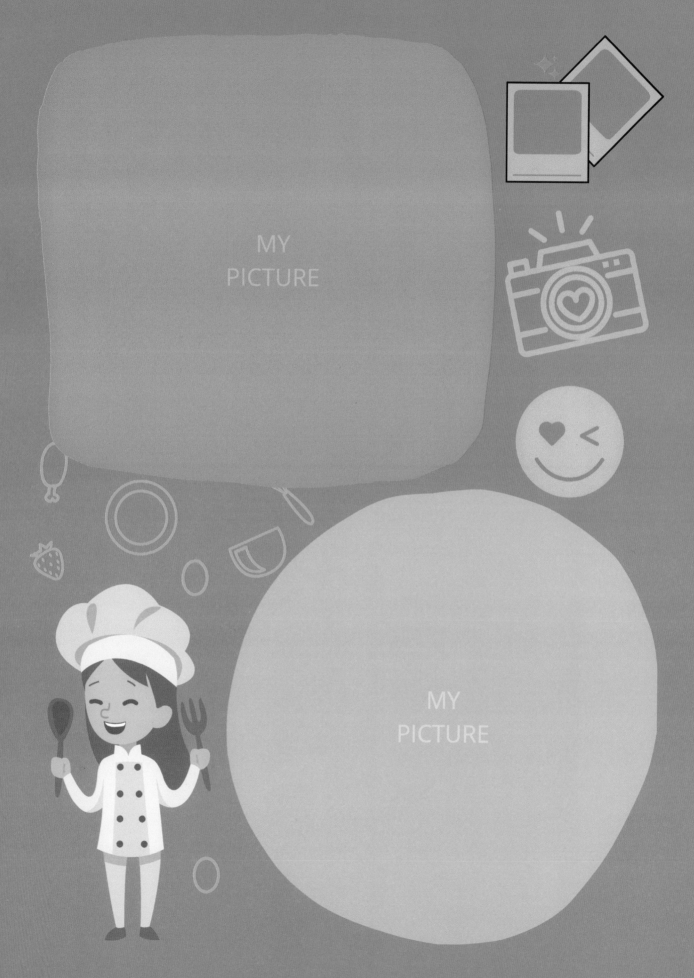

MY
PICTURE

MY
PICTURE

Printed in Great Britain
by Amazon

13509597R10045

CAN I COK by MYSELF?

RECIPES

Egg **TARTLETS** p.10
Couscous **TOMATOES** p.14
Ricotta&Spinach p.20 **CANNELLONI**

Mozzarella in **CARROZZA** p.26
Baked **RISOTTINI** p.30
Baked **POTATOES** p.36

Trofie pasta with **PESTO** p.40
Zucchini **PUFF PASTRY** p.46
Crispy **ASPARAGUS** p.50

Fantasy **ROLLS** p.56
Chocolate **SALAMI** p.60
Fruit **CAKE** p.66

- 12 simple, tasty and personalised vegetarian recipes to be made by children on their own from 4 upwards **+4**

- Simple illustrated guide with visual language, photos and drawings to make it easy to follow the steps and ingredients to use.

- Fun food games are included within the book.

Francesca MUSCI
Architect and digital marketing specialist but above all mom in love with her son.

Gabriel Marco LONGATO
A cheerful and curious child who loves adventures and new challenges. An inexhaustible source of joy and inspiration